To Carol
from Carol

All the best on
your Journey

Janice
Springer

Copyright© 2021 by Janice Springer

All rights reserved. No part of this publication may be reproduced, stored, or transmitted in any form or by any means without written permission of the author, except in the case of brief quotations embodied in critical articles and reviews.

Published by ShinrinyokuSanctuary

www.shinrinyokusanctuary.com

contact: Jdspringer2020@gmail.com

Cover and back photo Janice Springer

Haiku by Janice Springer

ISBN 978-1-7374678-0-9 (paperback)

ISBN 978-1-7374678-1-6 (e-book)

Printed in the United States of America

Table of Contents

Early Days	8-14
Friends	15-29
Turning Points	30-40
Gone	41-56

Preface

My life journey has provided me with countless days living in or on the edge of nature. The forest, trees, birds, all of it became part of how I interpret the world inside me. She gave me a pathway to take the feelings I had and make them visible, and over the years, shareable. I am fortunate to have many readers who urged me often to get published. Thank you all, I hope this work brings what you saw, what I felt, into the hands and hearts of those who need it.

July 2021

This book is dedicated to Billy

Early Days

Tiptoe through the fog
Uncertainty a promise
Last steps of aging

Days of Celebration

We have been granted
Extra days,
Thanks to the miracles
Wrought by
The Medical Industrial Complex
And its multiple layers
Doctors, Nurses, appointments
Medications, surgery
More appointments.

A brace, and grace.
We fly no balloons
Toot no horns or
Set off fireworks,
But we do gently
Touch hands
Slowly dance in the kitchen
Smile over a shared
Glass of wine
And revel in the gift
Of more days

Spoons

Lying here
Breathing soft
Tight skin to skin
In familiar spoons

A shudder passes
Through me as I
Remember that you
Are seventy now.

The actuarial tables
Are not that hopeful
For many more years
Of our bliss.

Kiss, and kiss again
Dance often, closely
Sunday morning mimosas
Awash with gratitude

Fragility Creep

When the guard is down
When the light is low
When the night has been long
Or the day an overflow,

I see the weary in your eyes
The weight of tired lines
I see the gnarled fingers curled
Protection from pain.

Millimeters at a time
Aging creeps along
Still, you have a dancing step
Still, you play a song.

Underneath this outer shell
Time is marching on
The clock is ticking, battery weak
Curtains will be drawn.

The Caregiver

Every morning, drowsy,
Sleep in her eyes,
Ready to greet the day
with joy,
She shrugs into the
undergarment of her life now.
It is heavy, but she keeps it
covered, with her bathrobe,
her flowing shirts,
her confidence.

Every day she puts in hours
of steady focus to lighten the load.
Coffee and walks with friends,
A good book, yoga,
Time in the garden,
Following her passions.

Yet in the evening,
she is so tired.
Even the one ounce
knitting needles lay
untouched.
Why am I so tired? She asks,

Wearing a garment only
she can see.

Deep in the Harbor

The largest harbor in this state
Is in our house.

The harbor of resentments
Has accumulated many boats
Floating just below the surface,
Easily retrieved,
Yet, under pressure
Sails are quickly opened
For a quick trip out to see/sea?
Where we can revisit a past journey
Rolling the bitter taste of old salt
Air in our mouth and seek
Restorative comfort
In the familiar of water.

Forgiveness

Forgiveness does
Not arrive like
A howling North Dakota
Blizzard. It drifts in,
One snowflake at a time
The early ones
Melt quickly on
Ground that is not yet
Receptive to
Its gentle cool nature.

It may take some time
Before enough slow
Lazy flakes have fallen
That a soft blanket of
White peace will
Stretch out before us.
And the dark soil of pain
Seems a distant season.

Friends

She smiles with each twirl

Alzheimer's in the background

He takes her dancing.

For Bill

Estranged from newspapers and radio,
I came late to the knowing,

Last night's blizzard with howling winds
And echo of musical tones in the chimney
Should have been a clue.
Bill, resisting to the end, going out with a howl
And a song,
Leaving us not quite ready for the void.

Your poetry had fastened itself to my heart
Some time back
Peering into Iceland through wise eyes.
Essays on islands, music and box elder bugs
Flavor our conversations like wine compliments
A good meal.

Out skiing today at 10 degrees,
Our cheeks as rosy as your normal Icelandic glow

A cheery part of your spirit,

Available in all seasons.

We will be "islanded" without your persistent

Connections pulling us out of ourselves

And into each others hearts.

Travel safe,

Your perpetual student

Bill Holm (1943-2009)

For John

I pull tight

A blanket of sadness

On this windy November day.

Not that the wind is

particularly cold

But the loss of a friend

Out of the blue

Compounded by my own

Aching joints

Has given me a shiver

Of fragility

That won't subside.

I seem to have migrated

To a demographic

Where life's tether

Seems to waver like the

Last leaf on the winter birch.

All I can do is reach out

To your soul mate

A sister nurse

A sister in widowhood

And offer the corner

Of my blanket.

John Tallaksen (1946-2015)

For Mary

When some unsuspecting

But kind soul,

Speaks of your

'Courageous' Battle

You will raise your fist in

Defiance -- saying,

It was not about courage,

It was a passion for living,

A furious determination

To keep bowling

To take more pictures,

To feast on friendships,

To ride my horse.

It was a fight not born of

Courage

But of steadfast resolve to

Be left standing tall,

Not relegated to the oxygen hose

And the wheelchair.

A fight of optimism over

Hard facts,

Of the joy of living

Over diagnostic categories.

Don't let them pigeon-hole you---

Leap on your horse Mary,

Ride fiercely to the east,

A camera slung across your side,

Blue eyes sparkling

And send us a post card

When you arrive.

Mary Lieberman (1927-2010)

Crossing Over

Our friend has made a crossing
This past six months,

He had planned to move
Gradually and with grace through
The potential minefield
But other plans were already
Under construction.

Age spots and
Striking grey hair were handled
With aplomb
Hearing aids came seamlessly
Into daily patter.

As one inches toward 80,
Nothing speeds the pace
Like chemotherapy.

Punted out of the league of
Dashing "young old" our friend

Has found himself teetering

On weak pins

Behind a walker

Looking "old old"

Straight in the eye.

Kind, soft spoken, well read

And articulate

Rocked completely free of his

Tethers by a body

Crossing over.

Leland Christenson (1931-2016)

Goodbye Friend

The black hood and scythe today

Are arriving in the form of a

Veterinarian in a truck.

They assure us she will be kind.

Meanwhile the clock ticks

As we hold him and wait

With damp eyes

And heavy hearts.

Spuds (1996-2006)

Immersion Therapy

Our ache is barely consolable indoors

Where the water dish is gone,

The special carpet where he lay, is gone.

His pillow by my bed, gone.

But out in the woods,

Drinking in the cool air,

Listening to the robins,

Navigating a snowbank

While hauling wood,

Our senses and our muscles

Give us a reminder of fond memories

Soaking up some of the pain.

Cone of Uncertainty.

We passed through a

Cone of uncertainty

This hurricane season

After the death of our best friend.

Unsure of where we would

Meet up with land

And break with the emotional winds,

We wandered through

South Dakota back roads

Seeking solace in the emptiness.

Long straight undulating roads

Left our minds free to

Soak up prairie gifts:

> Ancient cottonwoods rising out of fog,
>
> A pheasant, the bison and
>
> Miles of sunflower fields so welcoming
>
> Faces turned toward the sun with open arms.

No phones, no CNN, no droning lawn mowers,

Just calling owls, prairie dog towns, whistling winds

And living stripped down.

Sleep, Walk, Read,

Kiss, Hold,

Drink wine,

Eat chocolate,

Breathe deep,

Count stars,

Make love,

Sleep again.

Finding at last a

Koan of Certainty:

In the emptiness, your heart can fill.

Turning Points

Lying on the floor
Overcome with grief for him
Cancer strikes them both

Cold Lips

Deaths cold lips
Brushed my cheek
Last week
While cold October Mornings
Left frosty memos on
Fallen maple leaves.

She whispered quietly,
"This could be your turn
Girlfriend",
Then made me wait
For the next appointment.

I wonder if the
Phone call people
Have any idea where
You go after they leave
Their cryptic messages
About repeat X-rays
And dark spots
On the film.

Bad Weather

A 5mm dark cloud is

Stuck in a low-pressure system

For the last few days

As I try to divert myself

From the news

That I need to repeat

The mammogram.

Breast Cancer

The downside of not being

The one in 10 women

Who get breast cancer,

Is that one morning while

You stand and turn in

Each direction,

10 of your friends out of

The one hundred

Do get it

And you spin dizzy to the

Floor

With grief.

Trying not to jump

The tears quiver

Standing on the precipice

Of the lift bridge

Over my heart.

Wanting to dive into

The river of ache,

No matter the depth.

Unaware if today is

A mere trickle

Or a coming flash flood.

They come unbidden

And have the hardest time

Stepping back from the edge

For a more proper day.

Lost Cord

Dark grey clouds

Have been hanging over

My left shoulder

All day.

Full of tears

I have not yet shed,

Heavy with an ache

Hard to describe.

Deep sorrow for my brother

Who met his life-changing

Event at age 52.

Motorcycle vs car;

Spinal cord lost.

Benazir

As it came across the airwaves
I felt it deep
Thousands of miles away
As if it were next door.

She bled out from a neck wound,
Yet the pains were in my stomach.

A burning pain of Why?
I have no Pakistani genes
But my blood runs red
With the right of people
To choose their leaders.

Final Days

Do I want to spend

The end of my days

In a clever euphemism?

Will Crystal Waters heal me?

Is there anything special at

Care-Age Estates?

Will I have a view of the Pine trees

At White Pine Senior Living?

Or a river at Stoney River to soothe

An aching heart?

I think I will skip the pretense with walls

And opt for the true value of

Mother Nature, where I know

What I am getting.

By a Thin Hair

The depth of my emotional cushion

Is the breadth of a single hair

Lying quietly under my hat

Most days,

But flailing with abandon

In gusts of uncertainty with the slightest

Provocation.

It will take a very small set of scissors

To unleash the hurricane of despair.

As I Age

I sense a

More powerful joy

Being wrapped

By nature.

Today the wind is

Throwing waves

Against the rocks

Below my window.

Clothing flutters

In the breeze,

I feel whole.

On a summer hike

The forest brings

Her arms around me

Soil and blossoms

Fill my senses

Mushrooms at my feet

I feel whole.

I can begin to glimpse

How elders might walk

Into nature, desert,

Ice, mountain,

Wrapped in a cloak

Letting sleep and time

Overcome them

When they are done.

They know,

Where they are whole.

Knowing Glances

We recognize one another
Catching a glimpse as we pass
Knowing.
Each of us carrying
A backpack of the weight of
Our aging and chronically ill.
We worry, we care for, we drive,
We feed, we check medications,
We watch them fail
Inch by inch.
We watch them disappear
Pound by pound.
We watch them weaken.

We are a team without a coach.
No playbook other than those
Who have gone before us.
No crystal ball to know when
It ends.

No way of knowing when the

Next pounds will drop into our

Backpack, where we will continue

To carry on

Shooting knowing glances as

We pass through this corridor

Of our lives.

The Club

Ordinarily, a club is working

To grow its membership.

Invitations, newsletters, events

They throw out the Welcome mat

With promises of how great you will

Feel as a member.

But as I watch this new member stagger,

Gently supported by family and friends,

Into the widow's club this week,

My fourth in as many months,

I ache for the day I may be so

Welcomed.

Gone

Heavy Granite Stone
Compensation for lost life
Only one day old

Easter Morning

The pond is eerily calm

In this Easter dawn

No Frogs,

No birds singing

No wind.

Two male mallards swim aimlessly

Not eating

Or Fighting

Or preening.

Last night we thought

The cacophony of ducks

Was a celebration

Of the Full moon

Alas, on the far shore

Lies a flurry of blood-tinged feathers

Iridescent green floating

Two bright orange feet

In the air.

She will not rise again.

Land Angels

On a journey

That most of us resist,

Ernie allows the

Land angels

To hold him

Until

We must reluctantly

Hand him over

To angels of a higher order.

Ernie Gunderson (1953- 2013)

Oceans

May the salt

Of our ocean of tears

Contribute to the

Buoyancy of the water

To hold our heads up

Long enough to

Regain our strength

To swim back

Someday

To the joy of the journey.

Existential Alone

Is what you face
A month after your love
Is gone.

There is no one who cares
If you check in.
No one is waiting to hear
About your day,
Or share a dinner,
Or let you bring them a beer,
Or cuddle into bedtime spoons.

So how do you find your place
In the world
Without unbearable sadness,
Without your guiding star?

His Coat

Today I ache

For your presence

In your absence.

I've seen you twice

This week

And long

To run to that image

And hold you,

But the Birch tree

Appearing dressed

In your coat

At 200 yards

Does not respond.

Rip Tide

The rip tide is pulling.

I live on a lake

Yet,

I fight to keep from

Being pulled out

To the sea

Of grief

And tears

And missing him

So much

And

Nowhere is the lifeguard.

The First December

After 40 days and nights
In the wilderness of grief
I awoke this morning
To a crisp High Desert
Sunrise.
A promise of relief,
Perhaps some clarity
Through immersion with
The gifts of geology
And solitude
Trying to find my way.

Solstice Promise

Tonight, I carry a candle

To carry me into tomorrow

Past the shortest day

Past the progressing darkness

Of the last two months

Of my aching heart.

Long nights punctuated by

An occasional magenta sunset

Or a peach sunrise,

Match the rhythm of

My wandering heart

in the desert of loss.

May this flicker of light

Take me safely through

To the next season

Of longer days,

To build strength of spirit,

Soften the sadness,

Allow the power of nature

And sun

To heal.

Lost at Sea

Our first date was a picnic

Up a river, on a boat

Our last trip home from the cabin,

Was with our kayaks,

To tuck them in for the winter.

You were the rudder of our ship

My dear,

I was the sail.

I caught the wind

Cheered us through rough waters

While you held strong

Keeping our compass heading

Even when the winds of your life

Were winding down.

Now I sit in the doldrums

On the ocean of my life

Floating, watching

For a seagull, For a sign

For a whisper of breeze

To help me sail,

Again.

Cardiac Rehab

The EKG and treadmill
Are not the only indicators
For a damaged heart.

There are more electrical
Connections than modern
Cardiology can repair.

The heart is beating
Right on time
And oxygen is being delivered
As expected,

Yet the pulse of passion
That carried me for 50 years
In my profession, was deeply
Entangled with the love
Of my life,

Both of you have gone.

Torn in Half

Neuroanatomy aside
My brain and heart
Have hijacked my eyes
With their own agenda.

Every day my left eye
Stands firm and dry.
On the side of pragmatism,
Planning and steady on
To solve problems of the day.

Every day the right eye
Taps into the heart,
To memories to loss,
And sends a steady stream
Of tears, unbidden
Unrelenting,
Down my weary cheeks.

My Sweetie

My sweetie sends me notes on wings
Of raven, eagle and cranes.
He whispers to me softly
In gentle autumn rains.

He caresses my face
In the wind on my cheek,
He comes to visit
At least once a week.

He shows up in stories
With family and friends,
With tag lines like,
What did Bill do *Then?*

These visits are nice
And touching and kind,
They provide bits of solace
To my aching mind.

Trying to accept that

All will just have to make do

There will never be another shot

At holding you.

William 'Billy' Dahl (1939-2019)

Acknowledgements

I would like to thank my faithful readers. There have been many over the years who encouraged me and welcomed the random poems that came their way from time to time. Linda Ebner Erceg, a fine editor who does not seek poetry in her reading, but always welcomed my writing, and found my voice resonating for her. Kathy Springer-Lechuga, my sister, who carries a life-long passion for the work of Elizabeth Kubler-Ross and is now putting her heart into hospice work. Margaret Voss, a reader who came to me through a poem that was used for the funeral of Mary (p. 22) and asked for more, cheering me on with each one. Kim Schmidt Moore who spent many days with me in the highlands of the Orkneys of Scotland and the deserts of Big Bend, giving me a safe space to live in my pain. To Carol Eickoff, Marly Keller, Mary Crimi, Kip Peltoniemi, Julie Hiemenz and many others who I must have missed, my sincere thanks for the time you took over the years to peek into my tender places, with kindness and support. My thanks to Marilyn McGriff who coached me through the publishing process. Thank you to all the families who allowed me to publish a tribute to their love.

Finally, a huge thank you to Bill Dahl, who recognized the part of me that loved nature, and joined me there for our whole life: Dog mushing in the Arctic, scuba diving in Belize, kayaking in Alaska, hiking, skiing, and living in our cabin in Northern Minnesota, you gave me love entwined with natures gifts, a balm which sustains me in this new chapter of my life. You will always be my friend.